QUARANTINE

CONFESSIONS

Brody McVittie

for you,
my
mercurial
melodramatic
muse

(Mid)
MARCH.

153,517 people infected and
5,735 killed

This COVID thing is starting
to look a little scary

like it's not just a "over
there" thing

This won't be so bad.

You move out, literally, the way
you moved out, figuratively,
some time ago.

The world goes crazy, COVID 19,
and I'm alone with my typewriter.
And my whiskey.

And my rampant, all-consuming
sadness.

What's the worst that could
happen?

APRIL.

887, 067 people infected
and 44, 264 killed

and masks in public and death-
stares at anyone who coughs

and i'm wishing you would have
at least given relative
isolation a chance

because isolating is about as
good for me as the whiskey i no
longer save for Saturdays.

leave well enough alone.

Soaked my machinations in
whiskey

and

the reservations i have for you
are relegated to the dinners
we'll never go to

again

just the name of some Kravitz
song

i sing to myself
on nights since
the night you decided
my machinations were a little
too much.

*and by the way, remember
dinners out?

Fuck you, COVID.

ALL YOU LEFT ME

(WHEN YOU LEFT ME:)

-my word

-my big ol' balls

-the words i use in the stories

i tell myself

about you and the reasons you

left me.

THE SUM TOTAL OF MY DAYS, LOCKED
UP AND LOCKED AWAY IN THIS
APARTMENT:

Rumination, Proclamation, and
other Self-Important Shit.

how sad is it

the pics i used to get were naked
now all i get
are vaguely colored
discolorations
on zoomed-in parts of arms;

and the scars you leave
don't stop there
losing big toenails
and memories

of times you used to
pleasantly tease me

instead of now
and the just-teasings.

the worst part of all this:

I have to go and get my own fucking groceries.

how have you been

-OH YOU KNOW

WRITING SONGS
ABOUT YOU AND
DRINKING MYSELF TO
DEATH.

MAY.

3.2 million people infected
and 233, 000 killed

and the mask i wear
maybe keeps out the particles
that could kill me.

But the particles i'm primarily
concerned with are the particles
you left around my apartment;

the particles my mask and my
Dyson and my rampant alcoholism
can't seem to get rid of.

FIRST-TEAM ALL-DESPONDENT.

i've picked up the pen

and put down the glass

between sips and

at least long enough

to tell you the kinds of things

that maybe could have saved us

in the telling.

my name

your lips

knife turns

love hurts

sweet sounds

split lips

12 rounds

love hurts

4 letters

best words

leave now

hurts worse

you're not gonna like
this

but drugs, am i right?

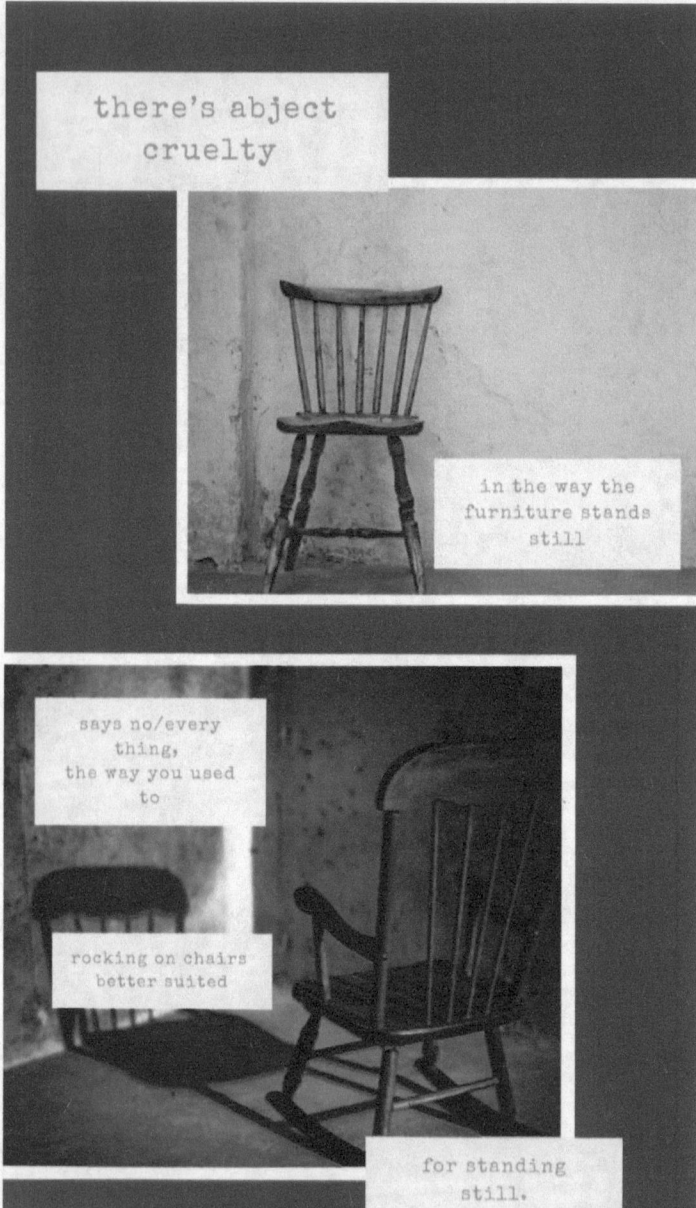

IF THE GOAL IS

BOOTLEG HEMMINGWAY

HOW MANY WHISKEY NO-CHASER
SPEAR-FISHING SAFARI
BAKING SODA INFUSED EIGHT-BALLS
BEFORE A MOTHERFUCKER GETS A SHRED OF

I GET IT.

I REMEMBER
EVERY/
NOTHING
ABOUT
THE
WAY
YOU
FORGOT
ABOUT
ME.

i'm waiting in line

outside the grocery store you
used to go to for me,

and i can't help but feel
that these groceries would be
better shopped sober

and i can't help but think
that, somewhere underneath this
mask i can't really breathe in

there's a face you might maybe
miss

the way i bet you don't miss

this waiting in line shit.

mom calls

the way you won't,

and asks how i'm doing...

Resplendently lonesome.
thanks for asking.

JUNE.

6.6 million people infected
and 375,000 killed

and masks are the new beards

(as in everybody's got one)

and my usually fashion-forward
ass

is bunkered up and decidedly not
on the beaches i should be.

(and you're still gone and the
even the weather isn't making
that okay.)

all

feels

smoke

&

semi-suicidal tendencies.

you pull off

GUCCI

FENDI

those mom jeans

i never thought would come back

yeah, you're well-dressed

but nobody wears

BROKEN

quite the way i do.

STILL

like time stands

and so i can count the colors in
the eyes

i caused the tears in

and

STILL

so i can take the time it takes
to take them all back

hold you with

eyes that tell you

i love you

STILL

and

you won't need the words

because my eyes will tell you

i

always

will.

Too many years
and the times time tends to
tell the stories we tend to keep
to memories of hot tubs and
the trouble hot tubs
tend to cause.

Behaving badly
because behaving badly
is what kids where we come from
tend to:

and in all the years
and all the times
the years tend to tell
the memories i have
of the secrets I'll keep

tell me you're just like me

trouble and too

two of a kind

and of the same mind.

Going for groceries
is getting downright dangerous

and they're out of both the
essentials
and the shit you used to find for
the counters

and so they're dirty,
the counters,

and the lines i resort to doing
off of them

are blurring the lines in my head

trying to remember why i gave up
personal shoppers/saviors
and the self-control that maybe
came with it/you.

Saying
"i don't know anyone who is sick"

is like saying

"i don't know anyone who is sick, yet"

but the isolation that comes

with not wanting to be

is likely making me sick, staying home and playing with straws

and sipping something i swear is medicine,

but maybe better suited for teething infants and sleepless tots.

i miss mom

and i miss dad

and i miss my baby sister

and her two babies.

i miss you,

but i think we've covered that

i miss not wearing masks

and i miss the me

that didn't have to

miss any of the above.

JULY.

10, 538, 577 people infected
and 512, 689 killed

and there's this Karen at the
kiosk at the mall

and she's yelling at me

about the type of mask i'm
wearing

because we're there now

and being here now,

kiosk at the mall

is the latest battlefield
July 2, 2020 has found me
fighting/losing on.

Today's Simple
    Truth

i miss you terribly.

HAVEN'T CHANGED
SINCE
SKINNED KNEES
AND
OVER-SIZED SWEAT SOCKS
(SO SIX)
AND
SO SORRY
I DON'T HAVE THE MATURITY
IT WOULD TAKE
TO NOT WRITE

EVERYTHING ABOUT YOU.

Funny how my drug dealer

is harder to get a hold of these days

but the drug dealer down the street

the one with the fucking neon

LIQUOR

sign

is about the only business open

(and business is booming.)

what should your
headstone say

HE NEVER STOPPED BEING SAD.

i've written the sentence
by the time the first word hits
the page

told the story

by the end of the first line.

i've finished the book
before the first paragraph.

i've read the first review
before i put the pen down.

i see the ending when i'm
beginning

because it is the only way

WORD ONE

ever amounts to anything

OTHER THAN.

baby, there aren't enough

Halsey songs

in the world

to tell you how disappointed i am.

what if i need you

to

save me

AUGUST.

17 million people infected
and lots dead.

 it's my birthday month and so
i'd rather not look at the
numbers.

you're calling, though, so it's a
little better than it has been,
on the whole painfully-selfish
scale i find myself (barely)
living in.

also, sun.

so that's good.

you call when it suits you

so not often

enough

for my admittedly tender/whiskey-
influenced

tender little sensibilities

and

the calls are short

and your tone is too

but in lieu of progress

i'll take it like that miracle vaccine
i'm pretty sure will never come to be.

you ask, and it's

Like, Lucas Hood sad.

and you get it, because he's
that guy from that show we
liked.

(*worth a google.)

you tell me that you're doing
good

and that's good

and, in passing, you tell me
that normal people don't go
grocery shopping every day and
that i can buy enough groceries
to last me, like, a week

and that's news to me

and i guess it kind of explains
why Karen at Checkout Station 5
keeps looking at me funny

also, fuck Karen.

my quarterback left

and

the government won't let
me go outside

and

i'm moderately sure the
world will never be the
same...

...and

none of this ruined me

the way you did

-inspiring the next/rest

every word and every

lack of

rest

with just one simple
call.

ABSCONDED WITH YOUR ATTENTIONS.

it's my birthday (!)

and it's a little different this
year and i don't feel like
celebrating

and there's a sick world outside
my window

and you're on the phone, which is
something

but i'm blowing out candles
metaphorically this year,

all isolated in august and
wishing

the work i'm putting into the
words

was working a little faster.

I REMEMBER WHEN

REMEMBER

wasn't a four
letter word.

why?

...because phantom pain

is the best pain.

SEPTEMBER.

26, 121, 999 people infected
and 864, 618 killed

and i'm shopping for the kinds
of things i hope will win you
back and

i think Karen is staring at me
but i can't tell,

her new mask is hidden by the
fogged-up face-shield she's
fogging up

and the kids are back to
school and decidedly not back
to school shopping

this year staying weird, all
empty malls and tactical-
looking kiosk operators.

FUNNY HOW I WAS EVERY

GOOD

FOUR LETTER WORD

AND THEN I WAS EVERY

BAD

FOUR LETTER WORD

AND NOW I'M ON MY BACK:

LIKE

LOVE

ME
,
FUCK

ME

... **CALL**

ME.

I THROW WORDS AT YOU

the biggest words i know
the smallest words with the
hidden meanings

words to boast about the man i am
words to hide the man i'm not

words that fall
deaf ears
unnecessarily parted lips

because the second i see you
the words i've said

mean nothing to the words
unsaid.

well, you know i'm always around
and willing to take it farther
than we maybe should.

WHY IS WAITING OUTSIDE AND IN LINE
AT THE LIQUOR STORE

NOWHERE NEAR THE PAINFUL
OF WAITING OUTSIDE AND IN LINE
AT THE GROCERY STORE?

3 Parts Hurt

2 Parts Whiskey

1 Part Disdain for the
basic nature of Self-
Preservation

...the perfect recipe for
the kind of doom girls
like you kinda go for.

YOU SAID
SEVENTEEN SOMETHINGS

TEN
SOUNDED KINDA SWEET

SIX
I REMEMBER EVERY SOUND OF

ONE
MADE ME FORGET FOR A MOMENT

THAT EVERY MOMENT WITHOUT

THE SOUND OF THAT SEVENTEENTH SOMETHING

WOULD RING IN MY EARS

LONG AFTER

PROVERBIAL RINGS LEFT SUPPOSED FINGERS.

I'M SOMEHOW BOTH

STAY AWAY

and

STILL

SYNONYMS IN THE HYMNS
YOU ONLY SING
TO YOURSELF.

i stay on pages

and

i never let go of anything

so

you're good, as far as

unrequited longings go.

so i'm equal parts

**get you back
don't die**

the way i have been
since corona was
just the beer i
passed in favor of
something stronger.

OCTOBER.

34, 495, 176 people infected
and 1, 025, 729 killed

and this is getting the kind
of old

that birthday back in August
tells me i am too.

YOU'RE THE KIND
WHO'S REALLY JUST NOT;

BLESSED WITH A BODY BETTER THAN

SOMEHOW LESS IN YOUR MIND

AND THE COST TO ME

AND MY INSATIABLE THIRST FOR THE
PICS THAT PROVE IT

IS DAYS WITHOUT MESSAGES
AND THEN MESSAGES WITHOUT NUDES

AND YOU IN THEM.

here's a little poem
i wrote you

corona is better when it's beer

and

life was better when you were here.

`SPOOKY`

LIKE HOW I'M ON YOUR MIND TONIGHT.

HAPPY HALLOWEEN

SINCERELY

-YOUR FAVOURITE GHOST.
THE ONE THAT HAUNTS YOU

(AND NOT JUST ON HOLIDAYS.)

GROWING UP I THOUGHT
GEORGE MICHAEL

WAS AS STRAIGHT AS A STRAIGHT MAN
GREW UP TO BE

AND

I MIGHT HAVE BEEN OFF ON THAT ONE

BUT

I'M ONE WHISKEY AWAY

FROM COMING OUT OF QUARANTINE

WITH A DANGLING CROSS EARRING

AND A PENCHANT FOR CHASING EVERYTHING
WITH DADDY ISSUES

LIKE IT'S 1987

cooped up
since
cooped up
was
coffee
and

cooked up
schemes
on how to get
cooped up
with
you.

locked up

and

the hurt is from

stubbed toes

empty fridges

you

the ghost in the graveyard
these four walls became
some days south of quarantine
still north of comfortable.

HAUNT ME

i'm proud of
the spiral i threw senior year

the car i stole to get to that party
(-*allegedly*)

the twist of tongue i could
form the words to fool you.

or girls like you
on some catchy pop song shit

because you
(and those cops back when)

never quite fell
for the sincerity i mixed

in and around the words to hide
the ways you terrified me.

SO THE LEAVES ARE TURNING
AND THE DAYS ARE GETTING SHORTER

AND THE LINES ARE GETTING LONGER

AND THE NEWS SAYS FLU SEASON MEANS
COVID SEASON, TIMES TWO

AND THE TIMING IS ALL WRONG, BECAUSE
I COULD USE MORE

TIME

TO WRITE THE REST OF THIS AND
BECOME THE KIND OF GUY THAT CAN
DRINK LESS AND SELL MORE AND

BECOME THE KIND OF FAMOUS
THAT I STILL THINK I DESERVE TO BE.

NOVEMBER.

46 million people infected
and 1.2 million killed

and there are rumblings of
lockdowns and restricted
movements and there's a good
chance everywhere but the
grocery store i begrudgingly
go to will be closed

again

and before the snow falls, i've
got to write the poem or say
the words that will get you
back.

because i'm tired of going for
groceries.

you said my name in my sleep

and my eyes opened.

i'm scared of
heights
rattlesnakes
covid-anything

i worry about losing
my mom
my hair
my semblance of the fragile ego i
cling to

since clinging to you
became something i just do
metaphorically now:

something i really want to
even though i'm really

most scared
of you.

Here's something better kept to myself:

you scheme with the subtelty of a
sound-cloud rapper

but when it comes to lies told with
twisted tongues

you're fucking with Annie Lennox.

educate yourself hoe.

There's no predictable pattern
to your errant unpredictability

and me and my
tender sensibilities
would prefer you not catching
my more embarrassing moments

in and around
the (only) moments
your errant unpredictability
chooses to
remember i made you that way.

BURNING BRIDGES WORSE THAN
DINNER

AND I CAN BLAME

THE BARBECUE
THE CHICKEN

YOU

ANYTHING OTHER THAN
THE TRUTH OF THE MATTER:

I COOK ABOUT AS WELL
AS I
CO-HABITATE.

i pay
compliments and for purses
paying for that one thing
i never really can:

prices north of
that last thing with all them zeroes
attached

all them

except the one i took
and on the chin

letting you close that door behind you.

Threw me under the bus
like i lined up against Bettis:

36 ways they did me
the kind of dirty that doesn't
come out of sheets

and between them
was where we lived before

rumors and rantings and
screenshots

blew me up harder
than
the drywall you put my coffee cup
through.

you remember
a laundry list of faults

respectable, mountain-sized
flaws

you fail to forget

i loved you

more than sweaters fresh out the
dryer.

you mind
a lot less than you think you do

and yours is filled
with the kind of dark

you swear my writing is too:

so we're the same
connected by the kind
that really kinda isn't

one reason
amongst the other 138
we can't stay away

the way you swear we need to.

DECEMBER.

61. 8 million people infected
and 1.4 million killed

Boxing Day mandatory
lockdowns

so Christmas isn't what it
used to/should be

and there's nothing under the
tree i don't have

and the chances of you
jumping out of a big, brightly
wrapped box are fading faster
than my sobriety.

♥   I STILL   ♥

like all your photos
and
i still
sing all your songs

and
not the way we used to
but

the tune i can't carry

weighs
way less than the baggage that weighs
and waits

by the door
you left yours by.

it's crazy

you can say
something

so simply:

send the sparks

behind the knees and
to chests

charge
that thing i try to
keep

locked up behind
(rib) cages.

TURNED YOUR WORDS INTO
W_INE...

AND

ALL I HAD TO DO WAS GET THE (H) OUT.

you swear you don't remember

and i swear i don't remember

but sunset car rides

have burned a place

in the memories that remind me

forgetting you was

something i swear i'll never do.

you're at least every-other thought,
and all of the restless ones

every late-night indulgence
and the sum total of my lost words
and misguided attempts at
explanation

you're things unsaid
and the soft parts i keep buried

but buried is only
until your eyes meet mine

and then you own them,
and the spaces between
leaving "other"

just another failed attempt
to think any thought unattached to
you.

Merry Christmas!

and it's really anything but this
year
because we're locked down starting
tomorrow,
and you're nowhere near willing to
come back to the place you ran from

so the presents under the tree
are just for me

and there's no need to wrap them
because they're really not there
anyways.

weekends go by
and you're anywhere else
and tonight's a Saturday
and that same bar is holding
you down

the way i used to.

so while you're collecting
attention
i'm catching the kinds of feels
it takes to write this,

one more page
until i'm done and famous

and everywhere else
but that same bar
that'll still be holding you
down.

764,260 vaccines administered
worldwide

some are excited, some are
skeptical; if being stabbed in the
arm means i can eventually roam
outside the constraints of my
four walls

i'll take the two i apparently
need to

and be back to making horrible
decisions regarding you

or girls just like you.

i came into this world ugly
and so i handle things the same

and meningitis couldn't kill me
the way that girl tried way
back when

so it's ugly but it works,
somehow
and i'm still here

although i apologize for the
way this starts

i can try my damndest to see it
doesn't end that way

if you'll wait me out
the way catastrophic childhood
diseases
and homicidal exes couldn't

i'm sorry

*christmas has me
all fucked up this
year.*

JANUARY.

80, 326, 479 people infected
and 1, 831, 703 killed

so Happy New Year!

(but not really)

because we were all hoping
the '1' on the end of 202_

would turn the page on this
shit,

and we'd be miraculously
cured and far better off

instead of the not better off

we so very clearly are.

climbing walls like cliffs
because imagination is outdoors, now

gone

the way of
favorite QB's on favorite teams

large gatherings

you

leaving me

to memories of outdoor spaces

championship runs

and

any hope of tomorrow being half the fun of the ones before

walls were cliffs

and

outdoors was something more than

something people speak fondly in remembrance of.

so your socials tell me
you're maybe seeing somebody new

/else

and as you can tell by the pages that
preceded this,

i'm clearly equipped to deal with it.

but hey,

New Year-New You

right?

i hate

settle

the way you hate

football

off-brand shoes

me

and i'm not mad you did

settle

so you have receding hairline him

and i'll keep

writing the words

that cause the storms

that still kill you.

words like

indifferent

will never be among the words
you feel when you feel things
about me

too many letters and too much
thinking of how to spell them

too much, taking away from the
thinking and of four-letter
words you'd rather

the way you'd rather just think
about me.

You're worth
the head trauma
and subsequent scars

the sleepless nights
and the ones i wish were,

dreaming it turned out different
and
waking up to

the marks i made
to remind me.

MORE BAGGAGE THAN TERMINAL 3.

♥ HEY ♥

i realize this reads fast

and i suppose last year went by the same,

locked up and longing

this year realizing you've maybe moved on

the way you moved out

some 117 pages ago.

*And i really should get over this,

but you're lingering like the pandemic

and i can't fully blame it

for keeping me from the outside world.

FEBRUARY.

102, 399, 513 people infected
and 2, 217, 015 killed

so Happy Valentine's Day!

(but not really)

because we're still locked
down and locked up

and it's way less fun in
winter,

and winter kinda feels like
it's never gonna end

the way COVID kinda feels the
same.

THIS MONTH FEELS A LITTLE ROUGHER THAN USUAL

AND THAT'S SAYING SOMETHING, AND I AM

AND I FIGURE IT'LL BE SPRING 2045

BEFORE I'M OVER THIS

THE WAY I'M OVER THIS.

Five million vaccines
administered worldwide

and whether you believe in them or
not, we're nowhere near getting one

because the shortages are
everywhere and the doses needed
are two

and one seems like it'll be forever

and the three, particularly
concerning variants have me
thinking

that as soon as there is hope on the
horizon

COVID kicks me right in the balls.

HELP, PLEASE

whiskey and worst behavior
hand in hand

metaphorically and maybe not
literally

but the vibe i'm putting out
there
because i can't be out there

is the kind of toxic
my liver most assuredly is.

Happy Valentine's Day!

and you ARE with someone new

and it's the not-okay it has been

but, in light of global events

and pandemics comma plural

i'll take it on the chin

and wash it down with something strong

and thank you for the best-seller you'll inevitably help me write .

ALL OF THIS IS EXHAUSTING.

tired of being

tired

maybe less rampant alcoholism
maybe more first-team all hopeful
because the former
resulted in a year wasted
and the latter
is all that's left.

the sun hits the snow
and everything kind of glows:
and it's minus one hundred something
but in lieu of darker days
i'll take the cold
over the closed-in
of closed-in rooms
and the thoughts that follow.

i'm at the grocery store
and

there's this girl in line
and

she doesn't smile like you

but she smiles, behind her mask
and

for the first time in forever

maybe

in line at the grocery store

isn't the worst thing in the world.

Lockdown is over (!)

for now, and i'll take it

Spring coming

Summer coming
(and over for dinner!)

Summer because that's her name

the girl from the line at the grocery store

the first of the maybe-good-for-me things i'll take to get over you.

(Mid)
MARCH.

lots of people infected and
too many killed

and for the first time in a
year, i'm not obsessing over
numbers

focused and on summer

summer in winter

the way it's been summer

since the fall

i fell for you.

you moved out, literally, the
way you moved out,
figuratively, a long time ago.

The world is still crazy,
COVID 19, but i'm not alone
with my typewriter anymore.

And my whiskey is rare now
and shared on occassion.

My sadness stays, sometimes,
and that's okay--because it's
no longer rampant and all-
consuming and always
directed at you.

The worst has happened,
and i'm still here.

BONUS

SOME MARCH IN THE FAR FUTURE

27.5 zillion infected and way
way too many killed

and you're married and you
have like 2.5 kids or
something

and you're happy and i'm

relatively

happy

relatively, because Bon Jovi
told me a long time ago that a
poet needs the pain

and COVID 239 keeps me somber
and motivated

the way you and the whiskey i
now stay away from

whisper to me from across
time and the places

time keeps whispering in my
good ear.

time heals all wounds.
*REMIXES

she said she thought about me

on her wedding day

and i don't have the clever

to turn the phrase

the way that particular knife does;

side

not worth showing

but rest assured

there's been little

just the thought that follows

the last thing she said

before words were ghosts

and days without weddings.

look, i'm not saying
those kids don't love you with
all their hearts...

...i'm just saying they don't love
you more.

i can only think of two things
you maybe love more than me

(and i bet it's still close)

because when you close your eyes
i can't think of one you see
in your mind and the dreams
you don't mind dreaming

the ones you have all the time
and still not even close

to how often i dream of you, too.

still

END.

*NEVER

www.ingramcontent.com/pod-product-compliance
Lightning Source LLC
Chambersburg PA
CBHW011318080526
44589CB00020B/2745